A LEGACY OF IVY, ROSES AND PEARLS

A History of Timeless Service of **Alpha Kappa Alpha Sorority, Inc.**
Phi Eta Omega Chapter—Scotch Plains, NJ

(1999—2013)

Order this book online at www.trafford.com
or email orders@trafford.com

Most Trafford titles are also available at major online book retailers.

Printed in the United States of America.

ISBN: 978-1-4907-5133-7 (sc)
ISBN: 978-1-4907-5132-0 (e)

Library of Congress Control Number: 2014921579

Trafford rev. 12/10/2014

 www.trafford.com

North America & international
toll-free: 1 888 232 4444 (USA & Canada)
fax: 812 355 4082

CONTENTS

ACKNOWLEDGEMENTS

This book is the result of many, many hours of research, many hours of re-writes, many hours of emails, and of course, many hours of input from sorors, Phi Eta Omega Chapter members of Alpha Kappa Alpha Sorority, Incorporated.

I wish to thank those sorors who initially agreed to work with me in this endeavor: Angela Driesbach, Joyce R. Hobbs, Michelle Lewis, Tynia Lewis, Grace Spivey Webb, and Drucilla Wiggins. An additional "thank you" goes to Carol Anderson-Lewis, Candace Pryor-Brown, Dewanna Graham, Jacquelynn Rhodes and Lyn Hamlin, our editor. Much appreciation goes to Kiabi Carson, Alison Bradshaw, Nicole Brightman-Beaton, Gail Reynolds, Bethany Andrade, Karen Andrade-Mims, Deana Lawson, and MaryAnn Anderson who worked to gather additional information. Finally, a special thanks to Angela Driesbach, Joyce R. Hobbs, Marjorie Hargrave, Jackie Turner and Candace Pryor-Brown for the use of their photos.

I give boundless gratitude to the chapter's president, Angela Driesbach and to the Scotch Plains/Union County Interest Group president, Drucilla Wiggins. Their help and encouragement have been invaluable.

Ann Troupe Thornhill, Historian/Archivist
Phi Eta Omega Chapter of **Alpha Kappa Alpha Sorority, Incorporated**

DEDICATION

Mary McLeod Bethune once said, **"Next to God we are indebted to women, first for life itself, and then for making it worth living."**

This history of Phi Eta Omega Chapter of Alpha Kappa Alpha Sorority, Incorporated is dedicated to the chapter's three "Golden Sorors": Rosetta N. Lattimore, Drucilla Wiggins, and Marilyn Lyde. These women have for more than 50 years dedicated themselves to the promotion of the high ideals of Alpha Kappa Alpha Sorority, Inc.

Reflections……..

Rosetta Lattimore - Soror Rosetta N. Lattimore became a member of Beta Rho Chapter at Shaw University, Raleigh, NC in 1948. Soror Rosetta recalls clearly how she first learned about Alpha Kappa Alpha Sorority, Inc. As she was preparing to attend Shaw University, a cousin visited her at home and wrote in her high school yearbook that she should join Alpha Kappa Alpha Sorority.

Once on campus, Rosetta had forgotten what her cousin had written. Yet, one group of women impressed her more than others. Of course, this group was Alpha Kappa Alpha Sorority. She admired their leadership, their concern and support for each other, and their service programs. These qualities that she recognized as a college freshman have sustained Rosetta as a member of Alpha Kappa Alpha Sorority, Inc. as well as in her life.

Drucilla Wiggins - Soror Drucilla Wiggins was drawn to Alpha Kappa Alpha Sorority, Inc. on the campus of Livingstone College, Salisbury, NC in 1957. She found these women to be quite influential on campus and exemplified outstanding leadership skills. Soror Drucilla became a member of Alpha Xi Chapter at Livingstone College in 1961.

Marilyn Lyde - In 1962 Marilyn E. Lyde became a member of Gamma Gamma Chapter at Morris Brown College in Atlanta, GA. Soror Marilyn is an acclaimed lyric soprano who has performed at St. Patrick's Cathedral, Carnegie Hall, and Madison Square Garden in New York City, The White House, and The Vatican for Pope John Paul. Like all sorors who bring their talents with them when they join Alpha Kappa Alpha Sorority, Inc., Soror Marilyn has used her voice to enhance the spirituality of the sorority.

IN MEMORIAM

".....Laugh as we always laughed at the little jokes that we enjoyed together. Play, smile, think of me, pray for me.... Why should I be out of mind because I am out of sight? All is well."

SEPTEMBER by Rosamunde Pilcher

Remembering......

Soror Jacqueline Arrington (2004)* Soror Jackie first became an Alpha Kappa Alpha member in 1991 in Nu Xi Omega Chapter. She was a charter member of Phi Eta Omega.

Soror Mary Lattimore Goldsboro (2008)* She became a member of the sorority in 1948 at Nu Chapter at West Virginia State College in Institute, WV. Soror Mary was a charter member of Phi Eta Omega.

Soror Clarie Minnis (2008)* Soror Clarie was the oldest member of Phi Eta Omega chronologically. However, you had nothing on her 90 years when she got behind the wheel of her RAV 4.

Soror Ogretta Whipper Hawkins (2009)* Soror Ogretta became a part of Psi Chapter, Benedict College in Columbia, SC. She was a charter member of Phi Eta Omega.

Soror Karen Wall O'Neal (2009)* Soror Karen became a member of Gamma Theta Chapter in 1983 and later became a member of Phi Eta Omega Chapter.

*deceased (Ivy Beyond the Wall)

INTRODUCTION

Ten inactive sorors of Alpha Kappa Alpha Sorority, Inc., rekindling a desire to be of service to others, assembled at a soror's home in Plainfield, NJ in the early winter of 1998. Soon this small group grew to fourteen and ultimately, to seventeen women. Later that year these seventeen women became, officially, the Scotch Plains/Union County Interest Group of Alpha Kappa Alpha Sorority, Inc.

With the mission to promote harmony and friendship among members, to develop and implement programs to enhance the self-esteem of youth, and to assist others wherever needed in the surrounding communities, these women ventured into "unknown waters".

Since its chartering on June 6, 1999, Phi Eta Omega Chapter has continued to institute and participate in the many altruistic programs: establishment of a weekly tutorial program, affiliation with the New Jersey Orators, "The Angel Network", "Dress for Success", financial support for two Kenyan school children, donation of filled duffel bags to Union County Division of Child Protection and Permanency and the replacement of the headstone of a Revolutionary War freed slave at Scotch Plains Baptist Church in Scotch Plains, NJ among others.

This book traces the history of the group from its inception as an official interest group of Alpha Kappa Alpha Sorority, Incorporated in 1999 until 2013.

Chapter 1

THE GATHERING OF SORORS 1998 -1999

**Drucilla Wiggins, President of Scotch Plains-Union County Interest
Group of Alpha Kappa Alpha Sorority, Incorporated**

Although I held offices and chaired various committees throughout the years, which helped to enhance my organizational and leadership skills, my greatest challenge was helping to establish the Scotch Plains/Union County Interest Group. As president, making late night phone calls, developing liaisons for community service projects, working with two regional directors, establishing protocol, and attending many, many meetings with members was, at times, exasperating. However, we prevailed; hence, Phi Eta Omega Chapter of Alpha Kappa Alpha Sorority, Incorporated became a reality.

Chapter One – The Gathering of Sorors 1998 -- 1999

INTEREST GROUP OF PHI ETA OMEGA

1998 – 1999

Under the urging of Soror Mary D. Williams, on January 7, 1998, a group of ten sorors; Carol Anderson-Lewis, Jacqueline Arrington*, Patricia Brokaw, Gail Cole-Spencer, Mary Gladden, Rosetta Lattimore, Margaret A. Lewis, Jacquelynn Rhodes, Mary D. Williams and Drucilla Wiggins assembled at the home of Soror Drucilla and committed themselves to forming an interest group to petition Alpha Kappa Alpha Sorority, Incorporated® for chapter status. The group chose the name: The Scotch Plains/Union County Interest Group of Alpha Kappa Alpha Sorority, Incorporated®.

The group organized and, shortly afterwards, mobilized four other members. Sorors Newana Barnes, Nellie Suggs, Ann Troupe Thornhill and Ogretta Whipper Hawkins* joined the interest group. On January 14, 1998 the group elected the following officers:

President -- Drucilla Wiggins

Vice President -- Margaret A. Lewis

Secretary -- Jacquelynn Rhodes

Financial Secretary -- Jacqueline Arrington

Treasurer -- Rosetta Lattimore

Hostess -- Mary Williams

Chaplain -- Nellie Suggs

The interest group met with Soror Wilma Tootle, North Atlantic Regional Director, at Freshwaters Restaurant, Plainfield, NJ on January 20, 1998. Soror Tootle and the group discussed the feasibility of creating a chapter in the Scotch Plains area. Subsequently, Sorors Adunni S. Anderson, Mary L. Goldsboro* and Joyce R. Hobbs also became a part of the chartering petition. Their goal was to establish an interest group in the

*deceased

Scotch Plains/Union County area to mobilize inactive and non-affiliated sorors, and ultimately, to become a graduate chapter of Alpha Kappa Alpha Sorority, Incorporated®. The mission of the interest group was to promote harmony and friendship among members and to develop and implement programs that would enhance the self-esteem of the youth in their communities.

The group developed a mission statement and identified community service programs under Alpha Kappa Alpha's international theme, "Blazing New Trails", ON TRACK. The interest group's signature program was to sponsor a NJ Orator's Chapter with St. John Baptist Church in Scotch Plains, NJ. The NJ Orators was an organization established to encourage minority youth, ages seven to eighteen years, to develop strong verbal and oratorical skills. The group established a weekly tutorial program (TAG) at St. John's to assist and strengthen the academic skills of the area youth. The interest group also chose to partner with the Foreign Missions Board at Shiloh Baptist Church, Plainfield, NJ. As a mission to assist the Christ Our Hope Maternity Home in Ghana, West Africa, sorors donated supplies and materials. Soror Edith Booker, the newly elected North Atlantic Regional Director, met with the interest group on December 12, 1998 at the home of Soror Margaret A. Lewis. Soror Booker reviewed the chartering application and discussed the required materials that were needed for submission to her and to the international office. Once the Directorate approved the interest group, the chartering had to take place within six months. The official approval of the chartering was given at the March 1999 Directorate Meeting in Freeport, Bahamas.

On June 6, 1999, the Scotch Plains/Union County Interest Group became Phi Eta Omega Chapter, the 128th chapter and the 67th graduate chapter in the North Atlantic Region of Alpha Kappa Alpha Sorority, Incorporated®. The chartering ceremony and luncheon was presided over by Dr. C. Edith Booker, North Atlantic Regional Director, at the Woodbridge Hilton, in Woodbridge, NJ.

Chartering of Phi Eta Omega of Alpha Kappa Alpha Sorority, Incorporated

The seventeen chartering sorors were; (L-R, 1st row) Drucilla Wiggins, Jacqueline Arrington*, Rosetta Lattimore, Margaret A. Lewis, Regional director Dr. C. Edith Booker, Ann Troupe Thornhill, Nellie Suggs, Adunni Anderson, Carol Anderson-Lewis, (L-R, 2nd row) Ogretta Whipper-Hawkins*, Mary L. Goldsboro*, Newana Barnes, Mary Gladden, Gail Cole-Spencer, Mary D. Williams, Joyce R. Hobbs, Jacquelynn Rhodes and Patricia Brokaw.

There was little time to enjoy the euphoria of becoming the 67th graduate chapter in the North Atlantic Region of ALPHA KAPPA ALPHA SORORITY, INC. The small group, under the leadership of Soror Margaret A. Lewis, as the first president, rolled up its sleeves and quickly went to work. There were certain programs already in place to continue and some new ones to inaugurate.

At Christmas in 1999, the chapter donated black dolls to the Plainfield Area YMCA Shelter. The following year, after Phi Eta Omega Chapter became a member of Jerseyland Park Community Center where its monthly meetings were held, the beautiful dolls were donated to the children who attended Jerseyland's annual Christmas party.

Chapter 2

A Beginning 1999 - 2001

SOROR MARGARET LEWIS, 1ˢᵗ Basileus of Phi Eta Omega Chapter

The formative years of any organization are usually a mixture of adventure, tremendous hard work, dissonance and optimism. Such was the case in the launching of Phi Eta Omega. Since I had previously served as basileus of my undergraduate chapter, Gamma Alpha, and a graduate chapter, Beta Pi Omega, I was well aware that the strength and success of any basileus depends, in part, on all members of the chapter.

It was with zeal that my sorors and I developed and implemented programs addressing the family, economics, education, health and the arts. We, indeed, set about "Blazing New Trails." Activities included sponsoring Scotch Plains Chapter of the New Jersey Orators, launching economic empowerment projects such as Black Dollar Days, planning the IVY ACADEMY at Jerseyland Park, presenting the first annual monetary scholarship/book awards and establishing the chapter's annual major fundraiser—the Cards and Games Scholarship Luncheon.

Chapter Two – A Beginning 1999 - 2001

The chapter's partnership with NJ Orators (St. John Baptist Church/Scotch Plains Chapter) continued for a 2nd year. Orators, ages seven to seventeen, held an audience spellbound as they delivered their orations at Barnes & Noble Book Store in Springfield, NJ in April of 1999. At the spring competition of 13 chapters and approximately 300 youth, Scotch Plains orators won 1st place for the group and four top individual prizes. Soror Grace Spivey's daughter, Nicole, received a perfect score. The final encore of the season was given at the Priory Restaurant in Newark, NJ where the orators were guests of the New Community Corporation. Among the pleasantries of the evening was the presentation of a Certificate of Recognition by the founder and Executive Director of the NJ Orators, Jim Hunter. Alpha Kappa Alpha Sorority, Incorporated®, through the sponsorship of the Phi Eta Omega Chapter, was the first and only Greek-letter organization to sponsor an orator chapter.

The year 2000 began with two sorors, Angela Driesbach Rose and Lyn Nickens Hamlin, transferring into Phi Eta Omega. Acts of volunteerism continued. Sorors participated as ushers at Crossroads Theater in New Brunswick, the first African American owned and operated theater in the state of NJ. Led and organized by Soror Jacqueline Arrington, Sorors Joyce Hobbs, Ogretta Hawkins, Jacquelynn Rhodes and Ann Troupe Thornhill volunteered on a bi-annual basis to support WBGO, NJ's only public/non-profit member-supported radio station. They contributed their time and talent as phone operators and tally masters, as well as accepted pledges and handled mailings during the station's fall membership drive.

Membership Drive at WBGO radio station in Newark, NJ

The chapter received a "Heart Grant" in the amount of $1,000 from the Union County Chosen Freeholders to support IVY AKAdemy. IVY AKAdemy provided arts and cultural programming for youth ages 14-17 in Scotch Plains. Young people were exposed to dance, songs, oratory, dramatic presentations and photographic exhibits. This initiative was led by Sorors Mary D. Williams, Nellie Suggs, Mary Gladden, Sharon Alsbrook, Grace Spivey, Yvonne Nambe and Margaret Lewis.

Numerous "acts of kindness" were carried out during Soror Margaret's tenure. Plants and cards were gifted to senior citizens of St. John Baptist Church in Scotch Plains. Additionally, the chapter instituted a new program, "The Black Angel Network", under the Black Family Corporate Target. "The Black Angel Network" was an adopt-a-family program. In collaboration with Metropolitan Baptist Church of Scotch Plains, the chapter identified a family of three boys, ages three, six, and eleven who were being reared by their single grandmother. Toys, clothes and food were donated throughout the year to support this family. In addition, an African American Literary Program was created in which books and CDs were donated to the Scotch Plains Public Library during the celebration of Black History Month. The chapter also participated in the nationally sponsored initiative, AKA IFresh Shoe Box Project. Shoe boxes were filled with school supplies and other multi-cultural educational materials for schools in Africa. On May 18, 2000, at Scotch Plains/Fanwood High School, Phi Eta Omega presented its first annual college book scholarships in the amount of $500.00 each to Christina Anne Hillman and Khalia Taylor.

In June, Phi Eta Omega's first anniversary was celebrated at the Spain Inn in Piscataway, NJ. On September 30, 2000 the chapter's first games/card party scholarship luncheon premiered. The revenue collected was for the benefit of scholarships. It was co-chaired by Sorors Grace Spivey and Mary D. Williams and was held at Café Piancone 2000 in South Plainfield, NJ. October was an active month for the chapter. Sorors walked in the American Cancer Walk-a-Thon in Newark, NJ and raised eleven hundred dollars for the cause.

Cancer Walk in Newark, NJ

Sorors continued to worship at least once a year as a group. In November the chapter worshipped at Metropolitan Baptist Church in Scotch Plains.

Sorors at Metropolitan Baptist Church, Scotch Plain, NJ

On December 9, 2000, Soror Ogretta Whipper Hawkins* presented a workshop on Alpha Kappa Alpha's protocol, traditions, and rituals. Phi Eta Omega's first Membership Intake Process (MIP) also occurred in December at the Holiday Inn in Springfield, NJ. The new sorors were: LeShaun Arrington, Learline Buckner Beaty, Carol Ann Brokaw, MaryAnn Anderson Fulmore, Monica Gallimore, Yvonne Nambe, and Candace Pryor.

1st Membership Intake Process, new members

Chapter 3

WE'RE ON OUR WAY 2001 – 2005

SOROR Joyce R. Hobbs, 2nd Basileus

Assuming the torch as the second Basileus of Phi Eta Omega, it was my honor to serve and lead the chapter into the new millennium with the transitioning of the new Corporate Signature Program, the **Spirit of Alpha Kappa Alpha.** In keeping with the corporate theme, my primary goal was to promote and foster the tenants of our great sisterhood. To attain this goal of retaining and reclaiming sorors, the following chapter programs were implemented: Secret Soror, Soror2Soror, and Sisterly Gatherings were spearheaded by the Hostess Committee. These activities included monthly repasts following chapter meetings, attending worship services, holiday luncheons and the distribution of a monthly basileus newsletter entitled **Phi Eta Omega**

Newsletter. Previously, a quarterly newsletter, **ASWALOS NEWS** (All Sister With a Lot of Soul), had been published. The chapter also sponsored its first reclamation event and a leadership retreat.

A secondary goal was to promote greater visibility in the Scotch Plains area. This goal was accomplished by participating in community service events such as the collection and donation of books to the Scotch Plains Public Library, participation in the Black Angel Network, donation of pajamas, clothing and books to children in need, and the educational sponsorship of two female students attending school in Kenya. The chapter embarked on the beginning phase of a major collaborative project that involved the restoration of Caesar's (a freed slave buried in the cemetery at S.P.B.C.) Gravestone with the Scotch Plains Baptist Church. This project was partially funded by a HEART Grant made possible by the Union County Historical Society. During my tenure as basileus, the chapter's visibility was increased not only within the Scotch Plains community but also with representation at the Cluster IV Basilei Council, Cluster Leadership, North Atlantic Regional Conference (NARC), Summer Leadership and Boule Conferences. On behalf of the chapter, I proudly accepted the regional (NARC) recognition award for timely completion and submission of the Standards Report, AKA Connection Report and Retention of Membership-Ivy Level. Phi Eta Omega also took the lead for Cluster IV at the Ivy Beyond the Wall/Worship Service at NARC in Atlantic City, NJ. The growth of the chapter membership was increased by the reclamation of two sorors and in February 2005 a new group of enthusiastic sorors, affectionately known as the "Loquacious Eight".

Chapter Three – We're on our Way 2001 – 2005

With the addition of seven enthusiastic sorors, Phi Eta Omega made great strides in carrying out programs already in place and in creating new ones. On the first Sunday in February, sorors participated in the African American Read-In sponsored by the National Council of Teachers of English. The national reading lists were distributed among the sorors who also shared their own lists with the group. Each participant shared a book(s) with the group, gave a brief synopsis and described why she enjoyed the book(s). Several sorors, who were educators, also planned this activity for their students as well. This activity, endorsed by the International Reading Association, created a chain of readers across the country and in addition, helped to promote sisterly relationships. The chapter continued to support additional reading programs by collecting and donating used books to the Scotch Plains Public Library. This was an effort to increase circulation of African American literature. Through Fountain Baptist Church in Summit, NJ, the chapter sponsored two African students by paying their tuition to the Isunguluni Primary School in Kenya. In the spring, the program committee designed an informational health workshop focused on diseases and health issues that impact commonly on Black women. Information was provided on diabetes, heart disease, high blood pressure and high cholesterol. The committee developed a handbook for each soror that outlined the causes for these diseases as well as suggestions for diet and exercise.

During this year Phi Eta Omega partnered with Links Inc. to develop educational workshops on organ donation and sickle cell anemia. These workshops were led by visiting Soror Gail Thigpen Allen. Chapter participation in "The Black Angel Network" continued. Sorors served as volunteer advocates in senior nursing homes and participated in breast cancer walk-a-thons as well as AIDS ministries.

In the fall, the chapter supported "Dress for Success/Back-to-Work" campaign by donating business suits and dresses for women exiting welfare and entering or re-entering the workforce. The annual card party to raise funds for scholarship support was held at The Westwood in Garwood, NJ.

Phi Eta Omega launched its first annual chapter retreat. The purpose was to provide a forum for reviewing chapter goals, objectives, sisterly relations, problem solving and to address the needs and interests of the members. Leadership development was an important component of the retreat.

For the holiday season, black dolls and toys were purchased and donated to the children of Metropolitan Baptist Church in Scotch Plains. In addition, food and clothing items were collected and donated to local food banks and community agencies that fed the homeless.

Christmas celebration and Black doll donations with Rosetta Lattimore & Orgetta Whipper Hawkins

Throughout the year, sorors continued to work with WBGO and were encouraged to support black-owned businesses and to keep abreast of newly established Black-owned businesses through the Black Dollar Days Initiative.

As a new millennium was getting underway, Phi Eta Omega continued its service to the surrounding Union County communities. Under the leadership of Joyce R. Hobbs, new programs were added to a strong platform already in place. The chapter continued clothing donations of women's suits to "Back to Work/Dress for Success" sponsored by the chain clothing store, Dress Barn. Our partnership with "The Angel Network" was sustained for a 2nd year. The chapter continued to support the single grandmother and the three grandsons that she was rearing. At Christmas the family was shown Phi Eta Omega's caring attitude with gifts and toys. In September at the start of the school year, book bags and school supplies were donated.

Our sponsorship of a chapter of the NJ Orators along with St. John Baptist Church of Scotch Plains, NJ continued to blossom with sorors serving as tutors and mentors. Seventeen Sorors participated in the 13th National African American Read-In on February 4 at Soror Lyn Hamlin's home in Somerset, NJ. The read-in offered a unique observance of a time honored tradition to read, reflect, and discuss significant literature of the African American culture and to define the impact on its status in post-civil rights America.

The chapter's annual activities continued. Seventeen sorors attended Founders' Day on February 23, 2002, along with other Cluster IV sorors at the Clarion Hotel and Towers in Edison, NJ. The 2002 North Atlantic Regional Conference was held in Uncasville, CT. At this conference, Soror Rosetta Lattimore was recognized as a fifty year member of Alpha Kappa Alpha Sorority, Incorporated®. Soror Lattimore along with Soror Mary Goldsboro became Phi Eta Omega's first golden sorors. Twelve of thirteen registered sorors were in attendance April 25-28 at our 71st NARC. Our delegates were Sorors Carol Brokaw-Boles, Joyce Hobbs and Jacquelynn Rhodes. Other sorors attending were Carol Anderson-Lewis, Jacqueline Arrington, LeShaun Arrington, MaryAnn Anderson Fulmore, Lyn Hamlin, Candace Pryor, Angela Driesbach Rose and Ann Troupe Thornhill.

Sorors with Rosetta Lattimore.

The annual card party/games fundraiser for scholarships was held September 7th at the Westwood in Garwood. Proceeds from this activity were awarded as scholarships to Sharee Bowles, a graduating senior at Scotch Plains/Fanwood High School and to Britanny Beazil, a freshman at Spelman College, Atlanta, GA, who was a scholarship recipient the previous year. Phi Eta Omega's sorors once again volunteered at NJ's only state public radio station, WBGO, during one of its membership campaigns. A re-activation activity was held at Soror Rosetta Lattimore's home on May 4, 2002. That same month, the group participated in the "Shoebox Project" sponsored by the sorority's international office. School supplies were again donated by the membership and packed into shoeboxes that were sent to a school in Africa. Through Fountain Baptist Church, Summit, NJ, the chapter once again sponsored two Kenyan elementary students.

As a sisterly relations activity, several sorors attended First Baptist Church of Lincoln Gardens in Somerset, NJ. A golf outing, "Chixs with Stixs", led by Soror Candace Pryor, took place at Scotch Plains Country Club on June 27th. Trial fundraisers were held at Chez Marie in Plainfield, NJ and on June 15th, a family picnic at Jerseyland Community Center celebrated Phi Eta Omega's anniversary.

After our regular chapter meeting on March 16th, a Leadership/Sisterly Relations Workshop was conducted by Soror Greta Shepherd of Beta Alpha Omega Chapter, Newark, NJ. On November 16, 2002 a sisterly relations retreat was led by Soror Lamyra Clark-White, former President of Beta Alpha Omega at the Scotch Plains Public Library. Our theme was "AKA is Alive in Me".

During 2001-2002 Phi Eta Omega's chapter meetings continued to be held at Jerseyland Park Community Center in Scotch Plains. Executive board meetings were held at sorors' homes or at the Scotch Plains Public Library. However, at the September meeting of 2002, the chapter took a serious look at location options for future chapter meetings. Subsequently, Phi Eta Omega's meetings were held at the Scotch Plains Public Library.

In December the year ended with the regularly scheduled chapter meeting and holiday luncheon. The two events were held at Maize Restaurant in the Robert Treat Hotel in Newark, New Jersey. Afterwards, sorors attended a Kwanzaa celebration at the NJ Performing Arts Center (NJPAC).

With the beginning of the new year, two sorors, Clarie Minnis and Brooke Tippins-Foster re-activated with Phi Eta Omega. Immediately embracing the chapter's momentum, Soror Brooke chaired the project to support one of the sorority's national projects, National Fire Prevention Week. The chapter purchased 25 smoke/fire alarms and donated them to Scotch Plains Baptist Church and to the Welfare Department of Scotch Plains. At February's meeting, a decision was made to seek an alternate venue for our executive board and chapter meetings. Newly re-activated Soror Clarie Minnis, a deacon at Scotch Plains Baptist Church, and Soror Jacquelynn Rhodes, a resident of Scotch Plains, were able to secure a new meeting place at Scotch Plains Baptist Church for October 2003.

February 2nd was the date chosen for the chapter's 2nd African American Read-In at Soror Lyn Hamlin's home. With continued emphasis on motivating the next generation, the chapter donated new or previously owned books which focused on the African American experience to the Scotch Plains Public Library. Additionally, the group received a service recognition certificate from the library for participation in its annual book sale. Sorors attended Pan-Hellenic Services at St. James A.M.E. Church in Newark, NJ on February 16th and ten sorors attended Founders' Day at Dolce Hamilton Park Conference Center in Florham Park, NJ.

Returning with valuable information, Sorors Joyce Hobbs, Candace Pryor and Stacey Anderson represented the chapter as delegates at the North Atlantic Regional Conference April 10-13, 2003, in Baltimore, MD. It was in 2003 that the chapter decided that its outreach for scholarship candidates would not only include seniors from Scotch Plains/Fanwood High School, but Phi Eta Omega should also reach out to Union Catholic and Westfield High Schools. The 2003 scholarship recipient was Raquel Romans. The chapter participated as a group for the first time at Relay for Life at Kean University in Union, NJ on June 6th and 7th. It was a celebratory and reflective event. Sorors fellowshipped and raised pledges totaling $1300.

Relay for Life at Kean University, Union, New Jersey

Phi Eta Omega prepared for its 2nd Membership Intake Process (MIP) designated for October 3-5, 2003. However, this weekend was cancelled and re-scheduled for January 2004. SuperKidz Camp was added as a new sponsorship for the chapter. This monetary support would allow a unique week-long camping experience in Northern NJ for an inner-city youth. 2003 ended with the December meeting and holiday luncheon at Georgiabelle's in Plainfield, NJ. This was also an opportunity to invite inactive sorors to join the group.

Phi Eta Omega welcomed the new year with a continued commitment of service to the residents of Union County. The chapter sustained its "Friends of the Scotch Plains Library" support by participating in its annual books sales and contribution of books by African American authors. In April, the chapter invited a speaker from the American Cancer Society to present a seminar on prevention and early detection. Several sorors volunteered to stuff envelopes for the Scotch Plains/Fanwood YMCA. The organization sponsored a community-wide "Ladies Nite-Out". Some sorors staffed a booth at the event. The event focused on health, financial planning and time management—issues that women must address daily. Eight sorors attended Founders' Day on Feb. 28 at the Bridgewater Marriott. They had the opportunity to be photographed with Supreme President Linda White and North Atlantic Regional Director Joy Elaine Daley.

Cluster IV Founders' Day at Somerset, NJ L-R(seated) Jacquelynn Rhodes, Clarie Minnis, North Atlantic Regional Director- Joy Elaine Daley, Supreme Basileus- Linda Marie White, Joyce Hobbs, Rosetta Lattimore, L-R(standing) Ann Troupe Thornhill, Orgetta Whipper Hawkins, Carol B. Boles, MaryAnn Anderson

Continuing the desire to have at least one sisterly church activity, several sorors worshipped at Soror Clarie Minnis' church, Scotch Plains Baptist on March 21st. Delegates for the 73rd NARC were Joyce Hobbs, Lyn Hamlin, and Candace Pryor. Also in attendance at the Downtown Philadelphia Marriott in Philadelphia, PA were alternates Angela Driesbach Rose, Carol Anderson-Lewis, and Ann Troupe Thornhill. Sorors Rosetta Lattimore, Drucilla Wiggins and Jacquelynn Rhodes joined the others during the March 11-14 conference. "A Sisterly Safari" was the theme of the May 23rd reclamation activity. It was held at Port Africa Art Gallery in South Plainfield, NJ. Good food and wonderful art exhibits were enjoyed by all.

The support of the KidzCamp initiative was continued and the recipient of the scholarship accepted the chapter's invitation to describe her summer experience at the monthly meeting. The two Kenyan Educational Scholarships were renewed and the chapter continued its contributions to Dress Barn's "Dress for Success". In the spring, scholarship awards were presented to Courtney Cook and Sonya Smith-Garner, students at Scotch Plains/Fanwood High School. Sonya was the recipient of the first Jacqueline Arrington Scholarship. The Arrington Award was created to honor Soror Jacqueline Arrington, who became "An Ivy Beyond the Wall" in April. In June, the members of the chapter had walked again in the "Relay for Life" at Kean University. It was a bittersweet occasion because Phi Eta Omega walked in memory of Soror Jacqueline, a charter member.

The chapter's 5th anniversary was celebrated at Vivace Café in Plainfield, NJ. During July 13-18, the chapter was represented by its President, Joyce Hobbs, at the 61st Boule in Nashville, Tennessee. After the summer recess, the annual games/card party for scholarships took place on September 13th at the Westwood in Garwood, NJ. Cluster IV's Fall Leadership Conference was held at William Patterson University in Paterson, NJ on Oct. 16th. There were several chapter sorors in attendance. As a conclusion to a very busy year, Phi Eta Omega celebrated with its annual holiday luncheon and donated generously to Toys for Tots in December.

As projects increased, fortunately, so did the membership. Sorors Christina Means and Poppy Elliott re-activated at the April meeting that year. In February eight new sorors were welcomed; Rachel Pereira, Tiffany Flewellen, Marjorie Hargrave, Kimiko Brightman, LaTanya Bennett, Sharon Giles Hamilton, Kimberly Brown and Cassandra Small. The MIP took place at the Holiday Inn in South Plainfield, NJ.

2nd Membership Intake Process

Sorors attended Cluster IV's Founders' Day on February 26th at the Taj Mahal in Atlantic City, NJ. The 2005 NARC was held at the Marriott Marquis in New York City. The delegates were Joyce R. Hobbs, MaryAnn Anderson Fulmore and Ann Troupe Thornhill. Sorors Carol Brokaw Boles, Ogretta Whipper Hawkins, Sharon Giles Hamilton, Candace Pryor, Rachel Pereira, Tiffany Flewellen and Marjorie Hargrave also attended. Alpha Kappa Alpha's Biennial Leadership Conference was held at the Atlantis in Paradise Island, Bahamas. Sorors Carol Brokaw Boles, MaryAnn Anderson Fulmore, and Joyce R. Hobbs represented the chapter.

In recognition of Women's History Month in March, Soror MaryAnn Anderson Fulmore presented flowers to Soror Rosetta Lattimore, a golden soror, and also to silver sorors. In 2005, Phi Eta Omega invited graduating high school seniors from Plainfield and Westfield to participate in the application process for the chapter's scholarships. Two scholarships were given that year; one of those recipients was Denise Horn.

As was customary, the group's anniversary was celebrated at the June meeting. It was the chapter's 6th anniversary and the celebration was held at Giovanna's in Plainfield, NJ. After re-assembling from the summer break, Phi Eta Omega held its annual scholarship luncheon at the Westwood in Garwood.

One of the chapter's important undertakings for the year was the replacement of the headstone of Caesar, a Revolutionary War freed slave, who had been a member of Scotch Plains Baptist Church. The chapter eagerly embraced this project and visited the gravesite in the adjoining graveyard of the church. A brief history about Caesar was give and the tour was guided by Rev. Chaz Hutchinson, the church's pastor.

Time Worn gravestone of freed slave Caesar at Scotch Plains Baptist Church, Scott Plains NJ

Afterwards, the chapter celebrated the 90th birthday of Soror Clarie Minnis with a brief repast of cake and punch.

Chapter 4

STRETCHING OUR LEGS 2006 – 2009

Carol Brokaw- Boles, 3rd Basileus

During my administration, the chapter had a successful audit. The chapter was able to revise its Manual of Standard Procedures and Constitution and Bylaws in conformity with the changes mandated by the sorority's international office. Phi Eta Omega hosted its first Leadership Conference in the fall of 2009.

The highlight of my tenure was the significant chapter presence at the Centennial Celebration of Alpha Kappa Alpha Sorority, Inc. in Washington, D.C. in 2008 where I had the privilege to sign the 100 year Legacy Book on behalf of Phi Eta Omega Chapter.

Chapter Four – Stretching our Legs 2006 – 2009

January 2006 began the tenure of Phi Eta Omega's third basileus, Soror Carol Brokaw-Boles. Many of the previous programs continued such as the celebration of Black History Month, Relay for Life and the chapter's collaboration with the chain store, Dress Barn. In observation of Black History Month, in February, the Sisterly Relations Committee organized a book swap of African American female authors. The following month, as another sisterly activity, Sorors Carol Anderson Lewis and Ann Troupe Thornhill shared with the group photos of their sorority activities during their collegiate days.

The chapter participated in the Union County Relay for Life event held at Roselle Park High School on June 3rd and 4th. The purchase of luminaries to honor Phi Eta Omega's Ivy Beyond the Wall, Soror Jacqueline Arrington, was spearheaded by Soror Poppy Elliott. In the same vein, a group of sorors, led by Team Captain, Soror Marjorie Hargrave, shared in the Making Strides Against Breast Cancer Walk at Military Park, Newark, NJ on October 13th.

The "Send-One-Suit" contributions to Dress Barn occurred in March and in October Phi Eta Omega participated in the "Divine Nine" coat drive hosted by Nu Xi Omega Chapter of Alpha Kappa Alpha Sorority, Incorporated® at Walmart in Piscataway, NJ. The 2006 North Atlantic Regional Conference was held March 29th - April 2nd at the Atlantic City, NJ Convention Center. The chapter was responsible for the Sunday worship service and the Ivy Beyond the Wall service.

The chapter's annual solicitation for scholarship recipients began in the spring. Soror Christina Means, scholarship chairperson, and her committee members presented recommendations to the group. Scholarship awards were given to Claudia Ahiabor and Denise Horn, who was a recipient the previous year. In May the chapter planned another fundraising activity to augment its annual scholarship card party/games luncheon. The "Spring Fling" Cabaret was held on May 5th at the Westwood in Garwood, NJ. The following September 30th was the date of the scholarship luncheon which was held at the same venue. Later in the fall Sorors Carol Brokaw-Boles, Drucilla Wiggins, Ogretta Whipper Hawkins, Learline Buckner Beaty and Mary D. Williams attended Cluster IV's Annual Leadership Conference at St. Peter's College in Jersey City, NJ.

The highlight of Phi Eta Omega's November chapter meeting culminated with the 2nd annual potluck Thanksgiving luncheon. Inactive sorors were invited to attend the luncheon. To complete the year the holiday luncheon was held at Carrabba's Italian Grille in Greenbrook, NJ. The chapter's "Soror Holiday Gift Swap" was held and books and toys were donated to Metropolitan Baptist Church in Scotch Plains, NJ.

During the weekend of February 18, 2007, Phi Eta Omega conducted its 3rd Membership Intake Process (MIP). The induction of nine members occurred at the Holiday Inn in South Plainfield, NJ. Those new sorors were: Nicole Brightman, Kiabi Carson, Dewanna Graham, Melinda Lawson, Michelle Lewis, Karen Andrade-Mims, Rosemarie Pena, Gail Reynolds, and Noni Robinson.

3rd Membership Intake Process

The new sorors were charged to create a chapter retreat which was held at Sherban's Diner in South Plainfield, NJ. Soror Lamyra Clark-While of Beta Alpha Omega Chapter, Newark, NJ was the guest presenter. Phi Eta Omega implemented a variety of Extraordinary Service Programs (ESP) such as participation in the American Cancer Society's Relay-for-Life, The Adopt-A-Family Project and the NJ CARES Annual Coat Drive.

The chapter's 2nd cabaret, a fundraising event for scholarships, was held at the Kenilworth Inn in Kenilworth, NJ in May. Scholarship benefactors of this event were Lauren Adams and Ariana Williams from Scotch Plains/Fanwood High School, Lovely Jean-Baptiste and Swhendhy Cantave students at Elizabeth High School and Tynia Lewis from Union High School.

The November meeting was held at Soror Learline Buckner Beaty's home in Colts Neck, NJ. At this meeting Soror Poppy Elliott presented a Health Resource Management mini-workshop on Breast Cancer Awareness. Afterwards, sorors enjoyed a Thanksgiving potluck dinner.

No matter where you were at the beginning of 2008, you were aware that "a change was a comin". This, too, was true for Phi Eta Omega. Foremost on Basileus Carol Brokaw Boles' agenda was the creation of an ad-hoc Technology Committee chaired by Soror Dewanna Graham. The committee's primary goal was to create a chapter website. As per previous years, the chapter continued with the officer and committee chair training and held another chapter retreat for the membership. The training session was held in January preceding the chapter's monthly meeting and the retreat took place February 9th at Giovanna's Restaurant in Plainfield, NJ. The presenters were Sorors Constance Pizarro, North Atlantic Representative to the International Membership Committee; El-Rhonda Williams-Alston from Theta Pi Omega Chapter; Drucilla Wiggins and Ogretta Whipper Hawkins from Phi Eta Omega Chapter. In February, the chapter welcomed the reactivation of Soror Nellie Suggs, a charter member, and in March, Soror Karen Wall O'Neal joined the sorors. Soror O'Neal had become a member of Alpha Kappa Alpha Sorority at Gamma Theta Chapter in 1983.

Phi Eta Omega continued its community based activities. Its first blood drive was in partnership with the American Red Cross and Scotch Plains Baptist Church on March 1st. The blood was donated to three area hospitals. Sorors Poppy Elliott and Nicole Brightman-Beaton chaired the drive. In April, once again, the chapter participated in the Send-One-Suit Initiative and collected 26 suits to be distributed to women returning to work. Also, members donated coats to the Divine Nine Coat Drive. The chapter helped advertise the Non-Traditional Entrepreneur's Symposium at Rutgers Law School in Newark, NJ. One of the symposium's presenters was Soror Karen Wall O'Neal. At the April meeting Soror Karen Andrade Mims conducted a Cancer

Awareness workshop which focused on screening, prevention, safeguards, diet and exercise. Again the chapter agreed to sponsor a youth at SuperKidz Kamp for the upcoming summer.

As customary, several sorors attended Founders' Day Celebration in February at the Doubletree Hotel in Newark, NJ. The 77th North Atlantic Regional Conference was held March 5th-9th in Philadelphia, PA. Delegates were Carol Brokaw- Boles, Drucilla Wiggins, Learline Buckner- Beaty, Sharon Giles- Hamilton and alternates, Joyce Hobbs and Marjorie Hargrave.

Since 2008 marked the 100th birthday of Alpha Kappa Alpha Sorority, Incorporated®, the chapter created a quilt square that was included in the NARC Centennial quilt displayed at the conference. Soror Sharon Giles- Hamilton volunteered to lead the chapter in designing its square. Also in conjunction with the sorority's centennial celebration, sorors participated in Cluster IV's 2 Mile Centennial Walk on June 28th in Morristown, NJ.

The "Spring Fling" cabaret was held May 2nd at the Kenilworth Inn in Kenilworth, NJ and the annual scholarship card party/games luncheon was held again at the Westwood in Garwood, NJ in September. The funds raised from these two events went towards the distribution of a scholarship to Ariana Williams, a previous recipient, and another to the chapter's first African American male recipient. Sisterly activities included a Thanksgiving potluck luncheon held at Soror Poppy Elliott's home in Somerset, NJ. Sorors organized and attended a reception at Rutgers University in New Brunswick, NJ for newly inducted Honorary Soror C. Vivian Stringer, Head Women's Basketball Coach at Rutgers University, New Brunswick, NJ. Lastly, Phi Eta Omega celebrated the conclusion of a successful year on December 20th with its annual holiday party at the Spanish Tavern in Mountainside, NJ. Sorors exchanged gifts and donated toys to the Union County Division of Social Service and children's pajamas were donated to an area hospital.

In 2009 Phi Eta Omega was 10 years old. It was still operating under the Exceptional Service Program (ESP). There were a few firsts this year: the first successful executive board conference call, the chapter's first time as host to the Cluster IV Leadership Conference, and the launching of the chapter's first website. Soror

Dewanna Graham worked diligently to create Phi Eta Omega's website along with Sorors Rosemarie Pena, Joyce Hobbs, Kiabi Carson, Angela Driesbach Rose and Marjorie Hargrave.

In line with corporate's initiatives, in March two mini-workshops were presented. Soror Karen Wall O'Neal presented "Financial Planning and Independence for Women" and Soror Gail Reynolds presented "Healthy Living". The chapter, in April, supported the Scotch Plains Fire House Department with a monetary donation of $25. Eight sorors participated in the Scotch Plains Relay-for-Life held at Scotch Plains High School and raised $500 in pledges. The annual scholarships were awarded to Ariana Williams from Scotch Plains/Fanwood High School and Janelle Zarelli from Union Catholic High School.

Phi Eta Omega continued to support the two elementary school children in Africa through Fountain Baptist Church and contributed to Super Kidz Camp with a $600 donation. In June sorors acknowledged the chapter's 10th anniversary by attending church services at St. John Baptist Church in Scotch Plains, NJ. Sorors socialized after the service with refreshments and all charter members were presented with flowers. It was also at this event that the chapter recognized charter member Mary D. Williams who was relocating out-of-state.

In 2009, the Central Jersey Pan Hellenic Council was re-established and Phi Eta Omega joined the council. Sorors Angela Driesbach Rose and Dewanna Graham actively represented the chapter. The Divine Nine Coat Drive was held in October and the chapter participated. Coats were donated to the Shiloh Baptist Church Clothes Closet in Plainfield, NJ and to Edison Job Corps. Led by Sorors Nellie Suggs and Grace Spivey, Phi Eta Omega re-affirmed its support of the NJ Orators at St. John Baptist Church.

The highlight of that year was Phi Eta Omega's hosting responsibilities of Cluster IV's Leadership Conference held October 10 at the Pines Manor in Edison, NJ. Soror Carol Brokaw-Boles was the chapter's basileus, Soror Joyce Hobbs was the chapter's chair of the conference and Soror Evelyn Sample-Oates was the North Atlantic Regional Director at the time. Sorors of Phi Eta Omega worked tirelessly in planning, in implementing and in ensuring that all sorors in attendance had an enjoyable and worthwhile Saturday.

Chapter 5

WE'RE ON THE MOVE 2010-2013

Angela Driesbach, 4th Basileus

It is a coincidence that the writing of this reflection coincides with my last month as the fourth basileus of Phi Eta Omega chapter. It seems like just yesterday it was spring 1987 on the campus of Tuskegee University. I was nineteen years old when I became a member of Alpha Kappa Alpha Sorority, Inc., Gamma Kappa chapter. Service, sisterhood, being a lady and lifelong membership were always emphasized as an undergraduate. It was then that I made a commitment to myself that I would always be financially active and would always provide service to all mankind.

Phi Eta Omega has worked tirelessly, diligently, and sisterly over the past four years to increase our visibility in Scotch Plains/Union County communities. We have worked with our youth, churches, and other non-profits implementing the Global Leadership through Timeless Service initiatives. Service has and always will be my primary focus in Alpha Kappa Alpha Sorority, Inc. I am proud to say that we have touched each initiative under the Global Leadership through Timeless Service platform.

One project that I am most proud is the completion of the Caesar Gravestone Restoration Project. The project was a huge success and brought the community together to learn about a former slave who resided in Union County, participated in the Revolutionary War as a wagoner, and worshipped at the Scotch Plains Baptist Church in Scotch Plains, NJ.

On a personal note, one of my most memorable moments was becoming a "Silver Star"—recognition of 25 years of service as an Alpha Kappa Alpha Sorority member.

Chapter Five – We're on the Move 2010-2013

The chapter reclaimed two sorors, Melinda Lawson and Nicole Brightman-Beaton. Under the Exceptional Service Program, chapters were asked to address issues related to non-traditional entrepreneurship, the economic growth of the Black family, health resource management, and the economic keys to success. In 2010, the members of Phi Eta Omega rose to the challenge of ESP with Every Soror (truly) Participating in a number of programs to benefit Scotch Plains and the surrounding communities.

The chapter began the year by honoring the legacy of Dr. Martin Luther King, J. The activity of the MLK Day of Service was to feed the homeless in Union County. The chapter assembled brown bag breakfasts that were donated to Bridges Outreach in Summit, NJ, an organization that has been serving the homeless for 25 years. This commitment to help less fortunate continued throughout the year with the chapter's collection and donation of clothing items to several organizations. In March, in recognition of International Women's Month, the chapter donated suits and other work-appropriate clothing to the Career Closet, a program run by the Junior League of Elizabeth-Plainfield that assists women making the transition into the workforce. In October the chapter participated in the annual Divine Nine Coat Drive by helping to donate approximately 200 coats to needy local families.

Brown Bag Preparation

Ever mindful of the importance of education, Phi Eta Omega has had a long tradition of providing programs that support student of all ages. Recognizing the importance of literacy for youth at an early age, the chapter annually participated in Children's Book Week – a national initiative dedicated to instilling a lifelong love of reading in children. In 2010 the chapter gathered books appropriate for elementary school children and donated them to the Scotch Plains Baptist Church Primary School in Scotch Plains, NJ. The group resumed its sponsorship of the Scotch Plains chapter of the NJ Orators with approximately 20 youth, some as young as seven years of age participated in the program. The impact of the Orators is evident in the numerous requests the students received to participate in local community events, as well as the chapter's success in local competitions. Phi Eta Omega proudly proclaimed a self-published author among its NJ Orators. One of the participants, a young lady, wrote a book and was invited to host book signings at several local book sellers.

As members of a sorority that places a high premium on education, the group supported several efforts to help local high school students attend college. The chapter sponsored a free ACT/SAT workshop for high school juniors. Offered by Kaplan Test Services and spearheaded by Sorors Joyce Hobbs and Dewanna Graham, the students were able to complete a mock examination and receive personalized instruction in their specific problem areas. In keeping with the sorority's focus on young Black males, the chapter underwrote the cost of two young men from Scotch Plains/Fanwood High School to attend a college tour to Morgan State University in Baltimore, MD. That same year, the chapter broadened its annual scholarship program to allow graduating Black males to apply for the awards. In that year, Phi Eta Omega awarded $3000 in scholarships to students from across Union County.

The year 2010 also marked the start of an annual service project with the Union County Office for the Division of Child Protection & Permanency (formerly known as the Division of Youth and Family Services). The organization was approached with the request to assist children who find themselves removed from their homes by the State, often with little or no notice. Under these circumstances, the children leave their homes with very little in the way of clothing, personal hygiene items, or the comfort of familiar toys or books. The chapter partnered with the Plainfield Chapter of Alpha Phi Alpha Fraternity, Inc. and several local companies to collect and donate duffel bags filled with items for these children. The twenty five empty duffel bags that had been received from the division were returned to the division completely filled. The community's response to this project was so overwhelming that the chapter had to purchase additional bags to hold the overflow items. In addition to the chapter's local efforts to support students, it continued financial support to a school in Kenya, Africa.

Christmas duffle bag distribution

Phi Eta Omega inaugurated its sponsorship of a health fair at St. John's Baptist Church in Scotch Plains, NJ. The health fair was designed to show that a healthy lifestyle was attainable. Information was provided in an informative and interactive way – helping to dispel some of the myths about living healthy. Attendees were able to sample healthy foods, showing that healthy food doesn't have to be bland and tasteless. They participated in several exercise programs, showing that you can exercise at home using items already in your home if your budget cannot support an expensive gym membership. To encourage attendees to commit to making healthy changes, the chapter sponsored a six week Women's Health Challenge, a project of the U.S. Department of Health and Human Services Office on women's health. Over the six weeks, members of the community joined with chapter members to modify their diets and implement an exercise routine. Participants received newsletters and other communications to keep them motivated. They also had the opportunity to participate in organized events to serve as further motivation. At the close of the challenge, all participants received a certificate of completion and those who demonstrated the highest level of commitment received special recognition.

The chapter also participated in several unique service projects specifically aligned with the aims of the ESP platform:

1. CERT Training: Members of the community joined with the chapter to complete CERT (Community Emergency Response Team) Training. In the wake of several emergencies and disasters and the overwhelming demand these events place on first responders, former President George W. Bush suggested that local citizens could be prepared to assist local first responders with specific tasks, e.g. triage and organizing victims, conducting light search and rescue, offering basic first aid, and aiding in fire suppression. Through an eight week program on emergency and disaster preparedness run by the Union County Office of Emergency Management, participants learned vital skills to assist themselves, their neighbors, and their communities in the event of an emergency or natural disaster.

2. Financial Literacy in Students: Recognizing that, too often, Black families do not properly educate their children on topics related to money, budgeting, credit, and making sound financial decisions, the chapter offered a workshop on financial literacy to high school students entitled " Your Money, Your Life". Over three months, students explored what it meant to make sound financial decisions and the impact unwise decisions can have on your future. For example, teens were encouraged to track their spending for a month. At the end of that month the teens determined which of the expenditures were "want vs. need."

3. Half the Sky: As part of a partnership with CARE, members of Alpha Kappa Alpha Sorority, Incorporated® were invited to raise awareness of the issues facing women living in impoverished parts of the globe. One such event was attending a presentation of the documentary "Half the Sky". This award-winning movie chronicled the lives of women living in patriarchal nations where women often are viewed as property or second-class citizens. It showed their determination to overcome their

circumstances, often at the risk of significant personal harm. The film hoped to enlighten the world to the plight of those women living in similar situations. The chapter participated in the worldwide screening of the movie in North Brunswick, NJ.

The chapter continued to walk at the annual Relay for Life at Scotch Plains High School. Family and friends shared in the walk and fellowship. Phi Eta Omega partnered with the Plainfield chapter of Kappa Alpha Psi Fraternity to have the first "Diamonds & Pearls Formal Affair" in May 2010. The chapters formed a committee and planned an elegant evening of dinner and dancing at the Hyatt Hotel in New Brunswick, NJ. The expenses and proceeds were divided equally between the chapters. There were at least 200 attendees in their finest attire. The chapter sold ads for a souvenir journal and gave each guest a wine bag as a favor to remember the event. The proceeds from the dance allowed the chapter to provide $2000 in additional scholarship money.

In September the chapter continued with the annual scholarship games/card party luncheon designating this annual event as the "Annual Rosetta Lattimore Scholarship Card Party/Luncheon". At the 2010 event there were at least eighty in attendance. One of the group's sisterly relations activities included dinner and a movie to see "Why Did I Get Married II". The sorors had a lovely afternoon at the movie and at dinner with family and friends.

The June meeting was held at Soror Rosetta Lattimore's home in Plainfield, NJ. To celebrate Phi Eta Omega's 11th anniversary, beforehand, sorors were asked to bring their favorite beverage with its recipe, if appropriate. After the meeting, sorors sampled the favorites of others. It was in 2010 that the chapter decided to focus on the completion of the "Caesar Project"—the restoration of a gravestone of Caesar, a freedman – that initially began in 2005. The group partnered with Scotch Plains Baptist Church and applied for the Union County Heart Grant to receive funds to help with the gravestone's restoration. Soror Jacquelynn Rhodes chaired the committee and worked tirelessly on the grant application. The grant was approved for $2000 and the chapter matched the grant to complete the headstone. "The Caesar Project" was a collaborative effort between Scotch Plains Baptist Church and Phi Eta Omega Chapter of Alpha Kappa Alpha Sorority,

Incorporated® to replicate the gravestone of Caesar, a freed slave who is buried in the church yard's historical cemetery. Salvageable remains of the original stone is encased and displayed inside the church. Soror Carol Anderson-Lewis and Pastor Chaz Hutchinson of the church met with a local stone mason, Lamperti, who designed the new headstone.

The "Caesar Project" has deep historical and educational value for the local and surrounding communities. Caesar was born in Guinea, West Africa and enslaved as a child. He was first owned by Isaac Drake of Plainfield, NJ who willed Caesar to his son Nathanial Drake. Nathaniel and Caesar were members of Scotch Plains Baptist Church. Caesar joined the church in 1747. As a slave, he was allowed to be a member of the church but was not allowed to serve as a deacon or hold any office due to the color of his skin. Caesar, however, continued his membership for over 50 years until his death in 1806 at the age of 104. He is buried near the Drake family's plot in the southeast corner of Mountain and Park Avenues in Scotch Plains, NJ. Upon his death in 1765, Isaac Drake's Last Will and Testament provided for Caesar's freedom. His headstone reads: "…it is my will and I do hereby order that my three Negro men as namely Tom, Caesar and Tone be set at liberty at the expiration of ten years after my decease and never after to be confined as slaves or as any part of my estate." This gave Caesar his freedom in his late sixties. In his seventies, during the Revolutionary War, Caesar served as a teamster, driving wagons pulled by horses to supply the Blue Hills Camp in Plainfield, NJ.

Upon the completion of the Caesar's Grave Restoration Project, Phi Eta Omega held a children's workshop, led by Soror Candace Pryor-Brown, to highlight the historical significance of Caesar. The following day, February 27, 2011, a gravestone unveiling ceremony was held at Scotch Plains Baptist Church. A program with guest presenters: Dr. Linda Caldwell Epps, Executive Director of NJ Historical Society; Ms. Ethel M. Washington, History Coordinator, Union County Office of Cultural Affairs and author of "Union County Black Americans"; and Dr. Leonard L. Bethel, Faculty-Department of Africana Studies, Rutgers University preceded the unveiling and a reception followed the unveiling at the grave site.

New Gravestone of Caesar, Scotch Plains Baptist Church

In 2011 Phi Eta Omega reclaimed Sorors Marsha Worrell, Gail Cole-Spencer, Alison Bradshaw, and Maureen Graham-Childs. One soror, Tynia Lewis, transferred and Soror Drucilla Wiggins became "golden". The chapter's focus shifted from ESP to "Global Leadership Through Timeless Service" (GLTTS). While some principles of GLTTS were consistent with areas where the sorority had previously focused its efforts, e.g. issues related to women and families, education, etc., this service platform also asked chapters to address new priority areas: Social Justice and Human Rights, a clear focus on health issues that disproportionately impact communities of color (asthma, kidney disease, diabetes), and the first ever signature program for middle school girls in Emerging Young Leaders.

Phi Eta Omega continued with several programs that had proven successful in prior years. The chapter again fed the homeless through its partnership with Bridges Outreach in Summit, NJ. Members participated in the annual Relay for Life event hosted by the students of Scotch Plains/Fanwood High School and raised thousands of dollars for the American Cancer Society. The chapter also completed the Duffel Bag Project to support children being monitored or managed by the Division of Child Protection and Permanency. Through this established relationship, Phi Eta Omega had the opportunity to participate in Union County's celebration of National Adoption Day. The chapter provided gifts and refreshments for 30 families who were legally joined through adoption on that day. In addition, the chapter awarded $3000 in scholarships to Bria Barnes, Lauren Williams and Ashley Romans, all Scotch Plains/Fanwood High School seniors.

Earlier in the year, the chapter was presented with an opportunity to support the Boys and Girls Club of Union by presenting the SMART Girls Program which was a part of the national curriculum for all Boys and Girls Clubs. Over a two month period the chapter met with approximately 60 middle school girls on a weekly basis to discuss some of the social and societal pressures that they experienced. Topics covered included self-esteem, bullying, personal hygiene, and age appropriate discussions on sexual myths that can cause young girls to make unwise decisions. At the culminating session, the SMART Girls created vision boards to show what they saw in their futures after having completed the entire program.

SMART Girls was a useful way for the chapter to gain valuable insight that was used to officially launch the Emerging Young Leaders (EYL) Program in the fall of 2011. Under the guidance of Soror Alison Bradshaw and other sorors, eight middle school girls from across Union County met monthly at the Washington Community School in Plainfield, NJ to explore the four areas of the EYL Program: character development, civic engagement, leadership, and academic excellence. The girls organized a canned food drive and invited the chapter to join them at Community Food Bank in Hillside, NJ to provide hands-on-service. The girls eagerly embraced the sorority's call to assist the military and their families by assembling care packages that were shipped to female members of the military on active duty. The eight participants in the program were Ayanna Abdul-Ahad, Heaven Hare, Farjah Huggins, Mya Jones, Ma'Sonia McPherson, Najhia Muhammad-Myers, Zariyah Salamea, and Zania Smith.

Building on the success of the inaugural health fair, the chapter took the lead in hosting this event in 2011. However, the location was changed to the Barack Obama/Green Charter High School in Plainfield, NJ. The theme of the health fair was the Black family-- with information and activities available for men, women, and children. In addition to traditional health-related information, attendees were able to receive information on topics such as safe sleep for infants, free or low-cost medical resources in the community, and sickle cell disease. Attendees had a chance to receive screenings for health issues that have a disproportionate impact on minorities, e.g. blood pressure, cholesterol, and the HIV virus. Because of the large scope of the event, Phi Eta Omega invited other local groups to join in implementing the health fair. As a result, Theta Phi Omega Chapter of ALPHA KAPPA ALPHA SORORITY, INC., Zeta Nu Lambda Chapter of Alpha Phi Alpha Fraternity, Inc. and the Plainfield/Scotch Plains and Bridgewater/Raritan Chapters of the National Council of Negro Women helped facilitate this SMART Girls program.

While the majority of Phi Eta Omega's service projects targeted the external community, there were times when the chapter implemented programs to support its members. For example, fortunate to have both physician's assistants and nurses among its members, Phi Eta Omega members received high blood pressure screenings, an educational program on the health risks associated with high blood pressure and information on how to combat the causes of this insidious disease after the May meeting, recognizing May as National High Blood Pressure Month. In June for National Cancer Survivor's Day, the chapter presented an ivy plant which represented strength to each chapter member who was a cancer survivor.

For the second consecutive year the chapter partnered with the Plainfield chapter of Kappa Alpha Psi, Inc. for the "Diamonds & Pearls Formal Affair" in May. This event again occurred at the Hyatt Hotel in New Brunswick, NJ. The chapters formed a committee chaired by Soror Jacquelynn Rhodes. There were 180 in attendance. The proceeds from the dance provided an additional $2000 towards the scholarship program.

In 2011 Phi Eta Omega participated in a tri-chapter social with the area chapters: Nu Xi Omega and Theta Phi Omega. Theta Phi Omega of Plainfield was the host chapter. The chapters met at Crescent Street Church in Plainfield, NJ for Sunday worship, brunch, and sisterly relations activities. Madame Regional Director, Constance Pizarro, was present at the gathering.

The chapter's June meeting and anniversary celebration was again held at Soror Rosetta Lattimore's home in Plainfield, NJ. The chapter's Annual Rosetta Lattimore Scholarship Card Party Luncheon was held in September at the Westwood in Garwood, NJ.

In 2012 Phi Eta Omega reclaimed two sorors: Charlene A. Lopez and Noni Robinson. Three sorors transferred into the chapter: Gloria Lyde German, Marilyn E. Lyde, and Jacqueline Turner. Marilyn E. Lyde became the chapter's third "golden soror" and Angela Driesbach Rose became a Silver Star (25 years) and a Life Member. The chapter's fourth Membership Intake Process (MIP) happily welcomed eight women in October. They were Bethany Andrade, Kelly Carmichael, Pamela Horn, Deana Lawson, Ashton Lattimore, Kalshelia Lloyd, Rena McClain, and Danielle Williams.

4th Membership Intake Process

Phi Eta Omega's service projects continued to improve the overall health and well-being of its members. In January each member was assigned a health buddy. The purpose behind the health buddy program was to encourage members to take care of each other, to remind each of the importance of scheduling routine physical examinations and to practice overall healthy behaviors. In addition, members with known health issues also were encouraged to follow up with the appropriate medical specialists to keep their conditions in check. In

March the chapter adopted dialysis patients at DaVita Dialysis Center in Kenilworth, NJ for Kidney Awareness Month. Patients received care and comfort packages filled with items to help ease the effects of their dialysis treatments. The month of May once again brought an educational program on stroke and high blood pressure.

The Emerging Young Leaders class, launched in September 2011, continued its monthly meetings. For the second half of the academic year, the EYL participants received lessons in etiquette and had an afternoon tea. They also learned valuable lessons about the dangers of social media and how to protect themselves in online settings. For Earth Day in April, the girls demonstrated what it means to "go green" by recycling old t-shirts and turning them into reusable shopping bags. In June, Phi Eta Omega congratulated three of the EYL participants for their graduation from the eighth grade.

The chapter expanded its programs in recognition of the Dr. Martin Luther King, Jr. Day of Service. In addition to assembling brown bag breakfasts for the homeless, the chapter hosted a Spa Day for residents at South Mountain Healthcare & Rehabilitation Center in Vauxhall, NJ. Residents were treated to manicures given by Phi Eta Omega members, the EYL girls, and other invited guests. Each resident who participated also received a small gift.

2012 saw the chapter implement its first program targeted towards the Environmental Stewardship and Sustainability focus area under the Global Leadership Through Timeless Service Health Initiatives. As part of the Membership Intake Process, members and candidates participated in a clean-up event at Echo Lake Park in Mountainside, NJ in partnership with the Union County Department of Parks & Recreation. Participants received a brief educational program about the park's natural ecosystem and what efforts were underway to preserve its natural environment. Armed with a newly acquired knowledge of invasive plants, the chapter cleaned the shore line of Echo Lake by removing the invasive plants and by picking up litter and other debris.

Earth Day Celebration, Clean up at Echo Park, Mountainside, NJ.

The chapter had its first "Pink Goes Red" Wine Tasting for the American Heart Association in February 2012 at the Wine Chateau in South Plainfield. All proceeds were donated to the American Heart Association. Another tri-chapter social was held at the South Plainfield Rescue Squad. This year the social was hosted by Nu Xi Omega with Theta Phi Omega and Phi Eta Omega sorors as guests. Each chapter was asked to bring food for tasting. There was a cooking demonstration by the president of Nu Xi Omega, Soror Rita Butler Holiday, and a wine tasting. In May the chapter and the Plainfield Kappas decided not to have a formal dance as done previously, but instead an "Old School Dance" was held at the Deborah Holmes Firehouse in Piscataway, NJ. All Greeks were encouraged to wear their respective paraphernalia.

The group's June meeting and anniversary celebration was held at Soror Candace Pryor-Brown's home in West Orange, NJ. Sorors brought their favorite beverage and appetizer or dessert. After the summer recess, the chapter resumed its yearly schedule with the Annual Rosetta Lattimore Scholarship Card Party Luncheon at the Westwood in September. Receipts from this occasion went towards our annual scholarship disbursement.

In November Phi Eta Omega participated in the Plainfield, NJ Feed the Children Program. Turkeys were purchased to help twelve families enjoy the Thanksgiving holiday. Through the chapter's membership in the National Pan Hellenic Council of Central Jersey, Phi Eta Omega adopted a family for the holidays and provided meals for Thanksgiving and Christmas. Chapter members recognized Thanksgiving by bringing their favorite desserts and shared them with the group.

In December, the chapter established a new relationship with Saint Joseph's Social Services Center in Elizabeth. Members helped to sort and assemble personal care kits for the families serviced by the center. During the chapter's time at St. Joseph's, over one hundred kits were packed for distribution. In keeping with its annual holiday tradition, Phi Eta Omega again partnered with the Division of Child Protection & Permanency to help children enjoy the Christmas season. Through this relationship with DCP&P, the chapter saw an opportunity to perform service under the Social Justice and Human Rights Initiative. During the holiday season, DCP&P receives numerous donations and gift items for their children. Most, however, are targeted to younger children, typically infants, toddlers, and /or those in elementary and middle school.

In 2012, the chapter adopted 40 high school youths being monitored by DCP&P as this age group is the most vulnerable during this season. The sorors generously gave gift cards, clothing and other items to demonstrate to these adolescents that they are not forgotten. This busy year concluded with the December meeting and holiday party being held at Due Mari Restaurant in New Brunswick, NJ.

The last year of Soror Angela Driesbach's tenure as president of **Phi Eta Omega** began with the chapter's January meeting being held at Westfield Town Hall, Westfield, NJ.

Observation of Martin Luther King Jr.'s Day of Service was a project centered around economic empowerment and youth. It was held in February in conjunction with the "Game of Life" activity of the chapter's Emerging Young Leaders. It was held at Bayway Family Success Center in Elizabeth, NJ. Eleven girls, grades 6-8, participated. It was a very positive event for all.

On February 2nd a "Pink Goes Red" Wine Tasting was held at the Wine Chateau in South Plainfield, NJ. All proceeds went to the American Heart Association. Also, sorors attended Cluster IV Founders' Day on February 16, 2013 in Mt. Laurel, NJ. Soror Evelyn Sample-Oates, Immediate Past North Atlantic Regional Director, was the guest speaker.

For the third consecutive year a Tri-Chapter Sisterly Relations Activity was held. **Phi Eta Omega** was the coordinator. The theme was "Pearl Sip and Twirl" held on March 16th at the South Plainfield Rescue Squad in South Plainfield, NJ. Although it was a snowy Saturday, the activity was well attended. Special kudos were bestowed to Soror Melinda Lawson and her committee. Soror Kelly Carmichael developed a specialty drink, Soror Melinda Lawson created microphone centerpieces and baked delicious cupcakes, and Soror Tynia Lewis led all in the spirited "karoke hour".

On April 6th Sorors Dewanna Graham, Alison Bradshaw, Michelle Lewis, and Tynia Lewis planned and implemented "The Princess in Me" fun-filled event for the girls of the Emerging Young Leaders. This activity was held at the Boys and Girls Club of Union, 1050 Jeanette Ave. in Union, NJ. It was a one day conference on self-esteem, self-respect, and self-image for girls in the 6th – 8th grades.

In April several sorors were in attendance at the 82nd North Atlantic Regional Conference in Philadelphia, PA. At this conference the chapter presented its first NARC display which was created by Sorors Joyce Hobbs, Dewanna Graham, Angela Rose, Lyn Hamlin, Deana Lawson, and Ann Troupe Thornhill. On May 4th the chapter and the Plainfield Kappas jointly held a cabaret at New Market Firehouse in Piscataway, NJ. Near the end of the month, May 25th, sorors and EYL participants donned their gardening gear and planted perennials at Warinaco Park in Roselle, NJ. as a deferred Earth Day celebration.

The June meeting was held at the club house facilities in Soror Lyn Hamlin's housing division in Helmetta, NJ. After the meeting the chapter celebrated its two new silver sorors, Maureen Graham-Childs and Joyce

Hobbs with a congratulatory reception. To complete the June activities before the summer recess, on June 29th Sorors Angela Driesbach, Dewanna Graham, Marjorie Hargrave, Michelle Lewis, Tynia Lewis, and LeShaun Arrington worked with Habitat for Humanity on a house at 1207 West Fourth St. in Plainfield. The sorors painted and installed laminate floors.

Habitat for Humanity

On July 17-21 Soror Angela Driesbach represented the chapter at **ALPHA KAPPA ALPHA SORORITY'S** Leadership Conference in Montreal, Canada.

After the summer recess, the chapter's activities resumed with the Annual Rosetta Lattimore Scholarship Card Party/Luncheon held on September 8th at the Westwood in Garwood, NJ. At the September chapter meeting it was noted that Sorors Danielle Williams and Joyce Hobbs had volunteered to be chapter ambassadors on the Cluster IV Sisterly Relations Committee. Soror Melinda Lawson, 2nd Anti-Basileus, and her committee recommended the establishment of a "Soror of the Year Award" and presented the criteria for the award. Soror Deana Lawson, the chapter's Educational Advancement Fund representative, reported on the successful brunch at Pines Manor in Edison, NJ. The "Salute to Excellence" Gospel Jazz Brunch occurred on September 14.

Other fall activities included the attendance of sorors for worship services at St. James A.M.E. Church in Newark, NJ for Panhellenic Sunday on October 27th and the chapter's participation through contributions with the Central Jersey Panhellenic Thanksgiving and Christmas "Adopt a Family". Finally, at the chapter's December 21st meeting, sorors again brought duffel bags generously filled with clothing, toiletries, books, etc. to be distributed to children under the supervision of the Union County Division of Child Protection and Permanency. After the meeting the chapter's annual holiday celebration took place at the same venue as the meeting, the Short Hills Hilton in Short Hills, NJ.

Phi Eta Omega has accomplished so much in its short period of existence. It has "blazed new trails" throughout many communities in Union County such as becoming the first Greek letter organization to sponsor a New Jersey Orators Chapter. It continues to be a chapter always on the move-- adding yearly new community programs for the benefit of others: the gifting of essential items to children in foster care, blood drives, distribution of smoke detectors and collection of suits and coats for women re-entering the workforce. The chapter has carried a "torch" illuminating the power of knowledge through education: providing scholarships to youth and educational experiences for all ages. The chapter, too, has understood the importance of holding steadfast to history—the completion of The Caesar Grave Project. The chapter has recognized that preservation of the environment is incumbent upon everyone—hence, the cleaning of local parks and planting of flowers to beautify the surroundings. The chapter has known the importance of "giving back"—by visiting rehabilitation facilities to remind the sick and elderly that they are not forgotten and by supplying labor for Habitat for Humanity. Full of hope for the future, Phi Eta Omega Chapter strives in this 21st century to advance and enhance the ideals upon which Alpha Kappa Alpha Sorority, Incorporated was founded.

2014 Phi Eta Omega of Alpha Kappa Alpha Sorority, Incorporated

APPENDIX A: Officers and Members Under the Leadership of Soror Margaret A. Lewis

Officers 1999

President .... Margaret A. Lewis
1st Vice President .... Joyce R. Hobbs
2nd Vice President .... Carol Anderson Lewis
Corresponding Secretary .... Mary S. Gladden
Recording Secretary .... Mary D. Williams
Treasurer .... Rosetta Lattimore
Financial Secretary .... Jacqueline Arrington
Hostess .... Mary Goldsboro
Keeper of the door .... Grace Spivey
Parliamentarian .... Ann Troupe Thornhill
Ivy Leaf Reporter .... Ogretta Whipper Hawkins
Chaplain .... Nellie Suggs

Membership 1999

Adunni Anderson
Newana Barnes
Patricia Brokaw
Gail Cole-Spencer
Jacquelynn Rhodes
Drucilla Wiggins

Officers 2000

President .... Margaret A. Lewis
1st Vice President .... Joyce R. Hobbs
2nd Vice President .... Carol Anderson Lewis
Corresponding Secretary.. Mary S. Gladden
Recording Secretary .... Mary D. Williams
Treasurer.. Rosetta Lattimore
Financial Secretary... Jacqueline Arrington
Hostess... Mary Goldsboro
Keeper of the door... Grace Spivey
Parliamentarian.. Ann Troupe Thornhill
Ivy Leaf Reporter .... Ogretta Whipper Hawkins
Chaplain .... Nellie Suggs
Historian... Jacquelynn Rhodes

Membership 2000

Sharon Alsbrook
Adunni S. Anderson
Newana Barnes
Patricia Brokaw
Gail Cole-Spencer
Lyn Hamlin
Angela Driesbach Rose

APPENDIX B: Officers and Members Under the Leadership of Soror Joyce R. Hobbs

Officers 2001

President .... Joyce R. Hobbs
1st Vice President .... Lyn Hamlin
2nd Vice President .... Jacquelynn Rhodes
Corresponding Secretary .... Carol Anderson-Lewis
Recording Secretary .... Carol Ann Brokaw
Treasurer .... Rosetta Lattimore
Financial Secretary .... Jacqueline Arrington
Hostess .... Ann Troupe Thornhill
Keeper of the door .... Grace Spivey
Parliamentarian .... Mary D. Williams
Ivy Leaf Reporter .... Yvonne Nambe
Chaplain .... Nellie Suggs
Historian/Archivist .... Ogretta Whipper Hawkins

Membership 2001

MaryAnn Anderson-Fulmore	Stacey Anderson
Newana Barnes	Learline Buckner-Beaty
Shae-Brie Dow	Monica Gallimore
Mary Goldsboro	Clarie Minnis
Angela Driesbach Rose	Candace Pryor
Drucilla Wiggins	Le Shaun Arrington

Officers 2002

President .... Joyce R. Hobbs
1st Vice President .... Lyn Hamlin
2nd Vice President .... Jacquelynn Rhodes
Corresponding Secretary .... Carol Anderson-Lewis
Recording Secretary .... Carol Ann Brokaw
Assistant Secretary .... Mary D. Williams (**)
Treasurer .... Rosetta Lattimore
Financial Secretary .... Jacqueline Arrington
Hostess .... Mary Goldsboro
Keeper of the door .... Grace Spivey (***)
Parliamentarian .... Ann Troupe Thornhill
Ivy Leaf Reporter .... Yvonne Nambe-Roach
Chaplin .... Nellie Suggs (**)
Historian/Archivist .... Ogretta Whipper Hawkins

(**) vacant after April 2002
(***) LeShaun Arrington replaces Grace Spivey after April 2002

Membership 2002

Sharon Alsbrook	Stacey Anderson
LeShaun Arrington	Newana Barnes
Learline Buckner-Beaty	Shae-Brie Dow
MaryAnn Anderson- Fulmore	Monica Gallimore
Mary Goldsboro	Clarie Minnis
Yvonne Nambe	Candace Pryor
Angela Driesbach Rose	Nellie Suggs
Drucilla Wiggins	Mary D. Williams

Officers 2003

President .... Joyce R. Hobbs
1st Vice President .... Lyn Hamlin
2nd Vice President .... Jacquelynn Rhodes
Corresponding Secretary... Carol Anderson-Lewis
Recording Secretary .... Carol Ann Brokaw
Assistant Secretary .... MaryAnn Anderson- Fulmore
Treasurer.. Rosetta Lattimore
Financial Secretary.. Jacqueline Arrington
Hostess... Ann Troupe Thornhill
Parliamentarian... LeShaun Arrington
Ivy Leaf Reporter .... Angela Driesbach Rose
Historian/Archivist .... Ogretta Whipper Hawkins

Membership 2003

Stacey Anderson
Newana Barnes
Learline Buckner-Beaty
Shae-Brie Dow
Brooke Tippens-Foster
Monica Gallimore
Mary Goldsboro
Clarie Minnis
Yvonne Nambe
Candace Pryor
Drucilla Wiggins
Mary D. Williams

Officers 2004

President .... Joyce R. Hobbs
1st Vice President .... Lyn Hamlin (+)
2nd Vice President .... Jacquelynn Rhodes
Corresponding Secretary... Carol Anderson-Lewis
Recording Secretary .... Carol Ann Brokaw
Assistant Secretary .... MaryAnn Anderson- Fulmore
Treasurer.. Jacqueline Arrington
Financial Secretary... Rosetta Lattimore
Hostess... Ann Troupe Thornhill
Ivy Leaf Reporter .... Angela Driesbach Rose
Historian/Archivist .... Ogretta Whipper Hawkins

(+) resigned June 2004

Membership 2004

Newana Barnes
Learline Buckner-Beaty
Brooke Tippens-Foster
Deborah Howard
Clarie Minnis
Yvonne Nambe
Candace Pryor
Drucilla Wiggins

Officers 2005

President .... Joyce R. Hobbs
1st Vice President .... MaryAnn Anderson- Fulmore
2nd Vice President .... Ogretta Whipper Hawkins
Corresponding Secretary.. Brooke Tippens-Foster
Recording Secretary .... Carol Ann Brokaw
Assistant Secretary .... Yvonne Nambe-Roach
Treasurer.. Jacqueline Arrington
Financial Secretary.. Rosetta Lattimore
Hostess... Carol Anderson-Lewis
Ivy Leaf Reporter .... Angela Driesbach Rose
Historian/Archivist .... Newana Barnes
Philacter... Ann Troupe Thornhill
Parliamentarian... Drucilla Wiggins
Chaplain .... Clarie Minnis

Membership 2005

LaTanya Bennett

Kimiko Brightman

Kimberly Brown

Learline Buckner Beaty

Poppy Elliott

Tiffany Flewellen

Sharon Giles- Hamilton

Mary Goldsboro

Lyn Hamlin

Marjorie Hargrave

Deborah Howard

Christina Means

Rachel Pereira

Candace Pryor

Jacquelynn Rhodes

Cassandra Small

APPENDIX C: Officers and Member under the Leadership of Soror Carol Ann Brokaw-Boles

Officers 2006

President .... Carol Brokaw- Boles
1st Vice President .... MaryAnn Anderson-Fulmore
2nd Vice President .... Carol Anderson-Lewis
Corresponding Secretary .... Angela Driesbach Rose
Recording Secretary .... Joyce R. Hobbs
Assistant Secretary .... Yvonne Nambe-Roach
Treasurer .... Jacquelynn Rhodes
Financial Secretary .... Rosetta Lattimore
Hostess .... Ann Troupe Thornhill
Ivy Leaf Reporter .... Kimiko Brightman-Archer
Historian/Archivist .... Newana Barnes
Parliamentarian .... Drucilla Wiggins
Chaplain .... Clarie Minnis

Membership 2006

Learline Buckner-Beaty
Kimberly Brown
Mary Goldsboro
Sharon Giles-Hamilton
Marjorie Hargrave
Glenda E. Jones
Rachael Pereira
Cassandra Small

LaTanya Bennett
Tiffany Flewellen
Dewanna Graham
Lyn Hamlin
Ogretta Whipper Hawkins
Christina Means
Candace Pryor

Officers 2007

President .... Carol Brokaw- Boles
1st Vice President .... MaryAnn Anderson- Fulmore
2nd Vice President .... Carol Anderson- Lewis
Corresponding Secretary .... Angela Driesbach Rose
Recording Secretary .... Joyce R. Hobbs
Treasurer .... Jacquelynn Rhodes
Financial Secretary .... Rosetta Lattimore
Hostess .... Learline Buckner- Beaty
Ivy Leaf Reporter .... Kimoko Brightman-Archer
Parliamentarian .... Drucilla Wiggins
Chaplain .... Ogretta Whipper Hawkins

Membership 2007

Karen Andrade- Mims	Newana Barnes
LaTanya Bennett	Nicole Brightman
Kiabi Carson	Poppy Elliott
Tiffany Flewellen	Mary Goldsboro
Dewanna Graham	Sharon Giles- Hamilton
Lyn Hamlin	Marjorie Hargrave
Deborah Howard	Rosetta Lattimore
Melinda Lawson	Michelle Lewis
Christina Means	Clarie Minnis
Rosemarie Pena	Yvonne Nambe-Roach
Rachel Pereira	Gail Reynolds
Noni Robinson	Cassandra Small
Ann Troupe Thornhill	

Officers 2008

President .... Carol Brokaw- Boles
1st Vice President .... Poppy Elliott
2nd Vice President .... Carol Anderson- Lewis
Corresponding Secretary.. Marjorie Hargrave
Recording Secretary .... Joyce R. Hobbs
Assistant Recording Secretary .... Yvonne Nambe-Roach
Treasurer... Angela Driesbach Rose
Financial Secretary.. Ann Troupe Thornhill
Hostess.. Learline Buckner- Beaty
Ivy Leaf Reporter .... Kimoko Brightman- Archer
Parliamentarian... Drucilla Wiggins
Chaplain .... Ogretta Whipper Hawkins
Doorkeeper .... Sharon Giles-Hamilton
Historian... Candace Pryor-Brown

Membership 2008

Karen Andrade Mims	LeShaun Arrington
Newana Barnes	LaTanya Bennett
Nicole Brightman-Beaton	Kiabi Carson
Tiffany Flewellen	MaryAnn Anderson- Fulmore
Sharon Giles Hamilton	Mary Goldsboro
Dewanna Graham	Maureen Graham-Childs
Lyn Hamlin	Melinda Lawson
Michelle Lewis	Christina Means
Rosemarie Pena	Rachel Pereira
Gail Reynolds	Jacquelynn Rhodes
Noni Robinson	Nellie Suggs
Karen Wall O'Neal	Mary D. Williams

Officers 2009

President	Carol Brokaw-Boles
1st Vice President	Marjorie Hargrave
2nd Vice President	Kiabi Carson
Corresponding Secretary	Dewanna Graham
Recording Secretary	Joyce R. Hobbs
Assistant Secretary	Karen Andrade-Mims
Treasurer	Angela Driesbach Rose
Financial Secretary	Ann Troupe Thornhill
Hostess	Learline Buckner-Beaty
Ivy Leaf Reporter	Carol Anderson-Lewis
Historian/Archivist	Candace Pryor-Brown
Philacter	Sharon Giles-Hamilton
Parliamentarian	Drucilla Wiggins
Chaplain	Ogretta Whipper Hawkins

Membership 2009

MaryAnn Anderson
LeShaun Arrington
Newana Barnes
Tiffany Flewellen
Lyn Hamlin
Rosetta Lattimore
Michelle Lewis
Yvonne Nambe-Roach
Rosemarie Pena
Gail Reynolds
Jacquelynn Rhodes
Grace Spivey
Nellie Suggs
Karen Wall-O'Neal
Mary D. Williams

APPENDIX D: Officers and Members Under the Leadership of Soror Angela Driesbach Rose

Officers 2010

President .... Angela Driesbach Rose
1st Vice President .... Dewanna Graham
2nd Vice President .... Kiabi Carson
Corresponding Secretary.. Jacquelynn Rhodes
Recording Secretary .... Joyce R. Hobbs
Assistant Secretary .... Michelle Matlock-Lewis
Treasurer.. Marjorie Hargrave
Financial Secretary... Ann Troupe Thornhill
Hostess... Learline Buckner- Beaty
Ivy Leaf Reporter .... Carol Anderson-Lewis
Parliamentarian.. Drucilla Wiggins
Chaplain .... MaryAnn Anderson
Keeper of the Door (Philacter)..................................... Sharon Giles- Hamilton

Membership 2010

Grace Anderson- Webb
LeShaun Arrington
Nicole Brightman-Beaton
Gail Cole-Spencer
Lyn Hamlin
Melinda Lawson
Rachel Pereira
Gail Reynolds

Karen Andrade- Mims
Newana Barnes
Carol Brokaw-Boles
Tiffany Flewellen
Rosetta Lattimore
Yvonne Nambe-Roach
Candace Pryor-Brown
Nellie Suggs

Officers 2011

President	Angela Driesbach Rose
1st Vice President	Dewanna Graham
2nd Vice President	Kiabi Carson
Corresponding Secretary	Jacquelynn Rhodes
Recording Secretary	Karen Andrade-Mims
Assistant Secretary	Michelle Matlock-Lewis
Treasurer	Marjorie Hargrave
Financial Secretary	Ann Troupe Thornhill
Ivy Leaf Reporter	Carol Anderson-Lewis
Parliamentarian	Drucilla Wiggins
Chaplain	MaryAnn Anderson
Keeper of the Door	Sharon Giles- Hamilton
Hostess	Joyce R. Hobbs

Membership 2011

Grace Anderson- Webb

Newana Barnes

Alison Bradshaw

Carol Brokaw-Boles

Tiffany Flewellen

Lyn Hamlin

Rosetta Lattimore

Tynia Lewis

Yvonne Nambe-Roach

Candace Pryor-Brown

Nellie Suggs

LeShaun Arrington

Learline Buckner-Beaty

Nicole Brightman-Beaton

Gail Cole-Spencer

Maureen Graham-Childs

Melinda Lawson

Marilyn E. Lyde

Rachel Pereira

Gail Reynolds

Marsha Worrell

Officers 2012

President	Angela Driesbach
1st Vice President	Dewanna Graham
2nd Vice President	Kiabi Carson
Corresponding Secretary	Jacquelynn Rhodes
Recording Secretary	Karen Andrade-Mims
Assistant Secretary	Michelle Matlock-Lewis
Treasurer	Marjorie Hargrave
Financial Secretary	Maureen Graham-Childs
Ivy Leaf Reporter	Carol Anderson-Lewis
Parliamentarian	Drucilla Wiggins
Chaplain	MaryAnn Anderson
Keeper of the Door	Melinda Lawson
Historian/Archivist	Ann Troupe Thornhill
Hostess	Joyce R. Hobbs

Membership 2012

Grace Anderson- Webb

LeShaun Arrington

Learline Buckner-Beaty

Nicole Brightman-Beaton

Kelly Carmichael

Tiffany Flewellen

Sharon Giles-Hamilton

Pamela Horn

Rosetta Lattimore

Tynia Lewis

Marilyn E. Lyde

Yvonne Nambe-Roach

Candace Pryor-Brown

Noni Robinson

Danielle Williams

Bethany Andrade

Newana Barnes

Alison Bradshaw

Carol Brokaw-Boles

Gail Cole-Spencer

Gloria Lyde German

Lyn Hamlin

Ashton Lattimore

Deana Lawson

Kalshelia Lloyd

Rena McClain

Rachel Pereira

Gail Reynolds

Jacqueline Turner

Marsha Worrell

Officers 2013

President .... Angela Driesbach
1st Vice President .... Dewanna Graham
2nd Vice President .... Melinda Lawson
Corresponding Secretary .... Tynia Lewis
Recording Secretary .... Karen Andrade-Mims
Assistant Secretary .... Michelle Matlock-Lewis
Treasurer .... Marjorie Hargrave
Financial Secretary .... Maureen Graham-Childs
Ivy Leaf Reporter .... Carol Anderson-Lewis
Parliamentarian .... Drucilla Wiggins
Chaplain .... MaryAnn Anderson
Keeper of the Door .... Jacquelynn Rhodes
Historian/Archivist .... Ann Troupe Thornhill
Hostess .... Joyce R. Hobbs

Membership 2013

Bethany Andrade

LeShaun Arrington

Newana Barnes

Alison Bradshaw

Carol Brokaw-Boles

Kiabi Carson

Sharon Giles-Hamilton

Pamela Horn

Rosetta Lattimore

Tynia Lewis

Gloria Lyde German

Rena McClain

Yvonne Nambe-Roach

Candace Pryor-Brown

Nellie Suggs

Jacqueline Turner

Danielle Williams

Learline Buckner-Beaty

Nicole Brightman-Beaton

Kelly Carmichael

Tiffany Flewellen

Lyn Hamlin

Ashton Lattimore

Deana Lawson

Kalshelia Lloyd

Marilyn E. Lyde

Monique Moore-Pryor

Rachel Pereira

Gail Reynolds

INDEX OF PHOTOS

New members not pictured: MaryAnn Anderson- Fulmore++ & Learline Buckner Beaty++.

- Photo #11   2nd Basileus: Joyce R. Hobbs

- Photo #12   Christmas celebration at a Plainfield, NJ restaurant. Rosetta Lattimore & Ogretta Whipper Hawkins are pictured with the sorority's Black doll donations.

- Photo #13   Celebration of Phi Eta Omega's first Golden Soror (50 years): Seated is the honoree, Rosetta Lattimore. (L-R, standing behind Rosetta)Ann Troupe Thornhill, Lyn Hamlin, Carol Brokaw-Boles, Jacqueline Arrington* (L-R, last row) Joyce R. Hobbs, Candace Pryor, Jacquelynn Rhodes, LeShaun Arrington, Angela Driesbach Rose, MaryAnn Anderson-Fulmore and Carol Anderson-Lewis.

- Photo #14   Relay for Life: Kean University in Union, NJ. Lyn Hamlin,, Jacquelynn Rhodes, Rosetta Lattimore and Joya, the clown (Joyce Hobbs)

- Photo#15   Cluster IV Founders' Day at Somerset, NJ: (L-R, seated) Jacquelynn Rhodes, Clarie Minnis*, North Atlantic Regional Director Joy Elaine Daley, Supreme Basileus Linda Marie White, Joyce R. Hobbs, Rosetta Lattimore (L-R, standing) Ann Troupe Thornhill, Ogretta Whipper Hawkins*, Carol Brokaw-Boles, MaryAnn Anderson-Fulmore.

- Photo #16   2nd MIP: (L-R) Kimiko Brightman, Kimberly Brown, Cassandra Small, LaTanya Bennett, Rachel Pereira, Sharon Giles-Hamilton, Tiffany Flewellen, and Marjorie Hargrave.

- Photo #17   Remainder of gravestone of freed slave, Caesar, at Scotch Plains Baptist Church: (L-R) MaryAnn Anderson-Fulmore, Ogretta Whipper Hawkins*, Carol Anderson-Lewis, Carol Brokaw-Boles, Rosetta Lattimore, Joyce R. Hobbs, Tiffany Flewellen, Candace Pryor, Rachel Pereira, Clarie Minnis*, Poppy Elliot, Jacquelynn Rhodes, Kimiko Brightman, Christina Means, LaTanya Bennett, Angela Driesbach Rose, Brooke Tippens-Foster, and Ann Troupe Thornhill.

- Photo #18   3rd Basileus, Carol Brokaw-Boles

- Photo #19   3rd MIP: (L-R) Michelle Lewis, Gail Reynolds, Nicole Brightman, Kiabi Carson, Rosemarie Pena, Melinda Lawson, Karen Andrade-Mims, Noni Robinson, Dewanna Graham.

- Photo #20   4th Basileus, Angela Driesbach Rose

- Photo #21   Preparation of brown bags for distribution

- Photo #22   Christmas duffle bag distribution in collaboration with Alpha Phi Alpha Fraternity: (L-R, 1st row) Candace Pryor-Brown, Michelle Lewis, Kiabi Carson, Drucilla Wiggins, Rosetta Lattimore; (L-R, 2nd row) Carol Anderson-Lewis, Dewanna Graham, Angela Driesbach, guest soror, Grace Anderson-Webb, Carol Brokaw-Boles, Marjorie Hargrave and Sharon Giles-Hamilton.

- Photo #23   New gravestone of Caesar: Jacquelynn Rhodes, Joyce R. Hobbs, Karen Andrade-Mims, Angela Driesbach, Lyn Hamlin, Kiabi Carson.

- Photo #24   4th MIP: Pamela Horn, Kalshelia Lloyd, Rena McClain, Danielle Williams, Ashton Lattimore, Kelly Carmichael, Deana Lawson, and Bethany Andrade.

- Photo #25   Clean-up at Echo Park, Mountainside, NJ in celebration of Earth Day:
(L-R, 1st row) Karen Andrade-Mims, Angela Rose, visitor, Michelle Lewis
(L-R, 2nd row) Deana Lawson, Ashton Lattimore, Kalshelia Lloyd, Tynia Lewis, Kiabi Carson, Tiffany Flewellen (L-R, 3rd row) Kelly Carmichael, Rena McClain, Pamela Horn, visitor, Bethany Andrade, and Drucilla Wiggins.

- Photo #26   Habitat for Humanity participation in Plainfield, NJ: Marjorie Hargrave and Michelle Lewis.

- Photo #27   2014 Phi Eta Omega Chapter of Alpha Kappa Alpha Sorority, Incorporated:
(L-R, 1st row) Jacqueline Turner, Michelle Lewis, Jacquelynn Rhodes, Tynia Lewis, Ann Troupe Thornhill (L-R, 2nd row) Melinda Lawson, Rosetta Lattimore, MaryAnn Anderson, Rachel Pereira, Drucilla Wiggins, Karen Andrade-Mims (L-R, 3rd row) Gloria German, Tiffany Flewellen, Carol Anderson-Lewis, Bethany Andrade, Deana Lawson, Rena McClain, Dewanna Graham, Danielle Williams, Gail Reynolds, Kelly Carmichael, Joyce R. Hobbs, Carol Brokaw-Boles, Nellie Suggs, Nicole Hines. **Not pictured:** Candace Pryor-Brown, Yvonne Nambe-Roach, Marilyn Lyde, Nicole Brightman-Beaton, Learline Buckner-Beaty, Angela Driesbach, Maureen Graham-Childs, LeShaun Arrington, Lyn Hamlin, Marjorie Hargrave, Kiabi Carson, Pamela Horn, Kalshelia Lloyd

GLOSSARY

Anti-grammateus .... Assistant secretary

Basileus .... Chapter president

Boule .... International conference, held

Biennially .... Every two years

First anti-basileus .... 1st vice president

Second anti-basileus .... 2nd vice president

Epistoleus .... Corresponding secretary

Grammateus .... Recording secretary

Hodegos .... Hostess

Ivy Beyond the Wall .... Deceased member

MIP .... Membership Intake Process

NAR .... North Atlantic Region

NARC .... North Atlantic Regional Conference

NARD .... North Atlantic Regional Director

Pecunious grammateus .... Financial secretary

Philacter .... Keeper of the door

Second anti-grammateus .... 2nd vice president

Soror .... Sister

Supreme Basileus .... International President

Tamiouchos .... Treasurer

BIBLIOGRAPHY

Bethune, Mary McLeod. "Mary McLeod Bethune: Inspiring Quotes from an Inspiring Woman." Accessed October 3, 2013. http://womenshistory.about.com/od/bethune/a/Mary-McLeod-Bethune.

Pilcher, Rosamunde, *September.* New York, New York: St. Martin Press, 1990. Kindle edition.

Walsh, Jeremy. "Erecting a (new) monument to a man of 'virtue and piety', " *STAR LEDGER NEWSPAPER,* November 28, 2010. 17, 20.

Washington, Ethel M. "In the Beginning". *Union County Black Americans.* Charleson SC, Chicago IL, Portsmouth NH, San Francisco CA: Arcadia Publishing, 2004. 17.

Printed in the United States
By Bookmasters